# Practical Pre-School

# Planning for Learning through Shopping

by Rachel Sparks Linfield Illustrated by Cathy Hughes

## Contents

Published by Step Forward Publishing Limited

St Jude's Church, Dulwich Road, Herne Hill, London, SE24 0PB Tel. 020 7738 5454

© Step Forward Publishing Limited 2008 www.practicalpreschool.com

All rights reserved. No part of this publication may be reproduced, stored in a retrieval system, or transmitted
by any means, electronic, mechanical, photocopied or otherwise, without the prior permission of the publisher.

Planning for Learning through Shopping ISBN: 978 1 904 575 17 7

 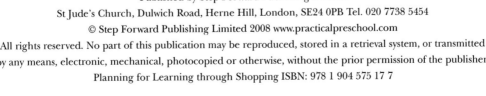

# Making plans

## Why plan?

The purpose of planning is to make sure that all children enjoy a broad and balanced curriculum. All planning should be useful. Plans are working documents that you spend time preparing, which later should repay your efforts. Try to be concise. This will help you to find information quickly when you need it.

## Long-term plans

Preparing a long-term plan, which maps out the curriculum during a year or even two, will help you to ensure that you are providing a variety of activities and are meeting the Statutory Framework for the Early Years Foundation Stage (2007).

Your long-term plan need not be detailed. Divide the time period over which you are planning into fairly equal sections such as half terms. Choose a topic for each section. Young children benefit from making links between the new ideas they encounter so as you select each topic, think about the time of year in which you plan to do it. A topic about minibeasts will not be very successful in November!

Although each topic will address all the learning areas, some could focus on a specific area. For example, a topic on Shopping would lend itself well to activities relating to Problem Solving, Reasoning and Numeracy and Knowledge and Understanding of the World. Another topic might particularly encourage the appreciation of stories. Try to make sure that you provide a variety of topics in your long-term plans such as:

| | |
|---|---|
| **Autumn 1** | Nursery Rhymes |
| **Autumn 2** | Autumn/Christmas |
| **Spring 1** | Weather |
| **Spring 2** | Shopping |
| **Summer 1** | Space |
| **Summer 2** | Farming |

## Medium-term plans

Medium-term plans will outline the contents of a topic in a little more detail. One way to start this process is by brainstorming on a large piece of paper. Work with your team writing down all the activities you can think of which are relevant to the topic. As you do this it may become clear that some activities go well together. Think about dividing them into themes. The topic of 'Shopping', for example, has themes such as 'Let's go shopping', 'Shopping for food', 'Shopping for clothes and shoes', 'Shopping for holidays', 'Shopping for birthdays' and 'At the DIY store'. At this stage it is helpful to make a chart. Write the theme ideas down the side of the chart and put a different area of learning at the top of each column. Now you can insert your brainstormed ideas and will quickly see where there are gaps. As you complete the chart take account of children's earlier experiences and provide opportunities for them to progress.

Refer back to the Statutory Framework for the Early Years Foundation Stage and check that you have addressed as many different aspects of it as you can. Once all your medium-term plans are complete make sure that there are no neglected areas.

# Making plans

## Day-to-day plans

The plans you make for each day will outline aspects such as:

- resources needed;
- the way in which you might introduce activities;
- individual needs;
- the organisation of adult help;
- size of the group;
- timing;
- safety;
- key vocabulary.

Identify the learning and the ELGs that each activity is intended to promote. Make a note of any assessments or observations that you are likely to carry out. After carrying out the activities, make notes on your plans to say what was particularly successful, or any changes you would make another time.

## A final note

Planning should be seen as flexible. Not all groups meet every day, and not all children attend every day. Any part of the plan can be used independently, stretched over a longer period or condensed to meet the needs of any group. You will almost certainly adapt the activities as children respond to them in different ways and bring their own ideas, interests and enthusiasms. The important thing is to ensure that the children are provided with a varied and enjoyable curriculum that meets their individual developing needs.

## Using the book

- Collect or prepare suggested resources as listed on page 21.
- Read the section which outlines links to the Early Learning Goals (pages 4–7) and explains the rationale for the topic of 'Shopping'.
- For each weekly theme two activities are described in detail as an example to help you in your planning and preparation. Key vocabulary, questions and learning opportunities are identified.

- The skills chart on page 23 will help you to see at a glance which aspects of children's development are being addressed as a focus each week.
- As children take part in the topic activities, their learning will progress. Collecting Evidence on page 22 explains how you might monitor children's achievements.
- Find out on page 20 how the topic can be brought together in a table top sale to involve carers, children and friends.
- There is additional material to support the working partnership of families and children in the form of a Home Links page, and a photocopiable Parent's Page found at the back of the book.

It is important to appreciate that the ideas presented in this book will only be a part of your planning. Many activities that will be taking place as routine in your group may not be mentioned. For example, it is assumed that sand, dough, water, puzzles, floor toys and large scale apparatus are part of the ongoing early years experience, as are the opportunities for children to develop ICT skills. Role-play areas, stories, rhymes, singing, and group discussion times are similarly assumed to be happening in each week although they may not be a focus for described activities. Groups should also ensure that there is a balance of adult-led and child-initiated activities.

# Using the 'Early Learning Goals'

Having chosen your topic and made your medium-term plans you can use the Statutory Framework for the Early Years Foundation Stage to highlight the key learning opportunities your activities will address. The Early Learning Goals are split into six areas: Personal, Social and Emotional Development; Communication, Language and Literacy; Problem Solving, Reasoning and Numeracy; Knowledge and Understanding of the World; Physical Development and Creative Development. Do not expect each of your topics to cover every goal but your long-term plans should allow for all of them to be addressed by the time a child enters Year 1.

The following section gives the Early Learning Goals in point form to show what children are expected to be able to do in each area of learning by the time they enter Year 1. These points will be used throughout this book to show how activities for a topic on 'Shopping' link to these expectations. For example Personal, Social and Emotional Development point 7 is 'form good relationships with adults and peers'. Activities suggested which provide the opportunity for children to do this will have the reference PS7. This will enable you to see which parts of the Early Learning Goals are covered in a given week and to plan for areas to be revisited and developed.

In addition you can ensure that activities offer variety in the goals to be encountered. Often an activity may be carried out to achieve different Early Learning Goals. For instance, during this topic children will share a shopping list and suggest ideas for where the things could be bought. Children will be using personal, social and emotional skills as they initiate ideas and speak in a familiar group. In addition, they will develop in the area of Communication, Language and Literacy as they recognise letters, attempt to read words, speak and listen. It is important, therefore, that activities have clearly defined goals so that these may be emphasised during the activity and for recording purposes.

## Personal, Social and Emotional Development (PS)

This area of learning covers important aspects of development that affect the way children learn, behave and relate to others. By the end of the Early Years

Foundation Stage (EYFS) children should:

PS1  Continue to be interested, excited and motivated to learn.

PS2  Be confident to try activities, initiate ideas and speak in a familiar group.

PS3  Maintain attention, concentrate and sit quietly when appropriate.

PS4  Respond to significant experiences, showing a range of feelings when appropriate.

PS5  Have a developing awareness of their own needs, views and feelings, and be sensitive to the needs, views and feelings of others.

PS6  Have a developing respect for their own cultures and beliefs and those of other people.

PS7  Form good relationships with adults and peers.

PS8  Work as a part of a group or class, taking turns and sharing fairly, understanding that there needs to be agreed values and codes of behaviour for groups of people, including adults and children, to work together harmoniously.

PS9  Understand what is right, what is wrong and why.

PS10 Consider the consequences of their words and actions for themselves and others.

PS11    Dress and undress independently and manage their own personal hygiene.

PS12    Select and use activities and resources independently.

PS13    Understand that people have different needs, views, cultures and beliefs, that need to be treated with respect.

PS14    Understand that they can expect others to treat their needs, views, cultures and beliefs with respect.

The topic of 'Shopping' offers many opportunities for children's personal, social and emotional development. Time spent discussing where things can be bought will encourage children to speak in a group and to be interested to learn. Buying and selling in a role-play shop or café and folding clothes to fit in carrier bags will encourage the children to consider consequences and understand what is wrong, what is right and why. Many of the areas outlined above, though, will be covered on an almost incidental basis as children carry out the activities described in this book for the other areas of children's learning. During undirected free choice times they will be developing PS12 whilst any small group activity that involves working with an adult will help children to work towards PS7.

# Communication, Language and Literacy (L)

By the end of the EYFS, children should:

L1    Interact with others, negotiating plans and activities and taking turns in conversation.

L2    Enjoy listening to and using spoken and written language, and readily turn to it in their play and learning.

L3    Sustain attentive listening, responding to what they have heard with relevant comments, questions or actions.

L4    Listen with enjoyment, and respond to stories, songs and other music, rhymes and poems and make up their own stories, songs, rhymes and poems.

L5    Extend their vocabulary, exploring the meanings and sounds of new words.

L6    Speak clearly and audibly with confidence and control and show awareness of the listener.

L7    Use language to imagine and recreate roles and experiences.

L8    Use talk to organise, sequence and clarify thinking, ideas, feelings and events.

L9    Hear and say sounds in words in the order in which they occur.

L10    Link sounds to letters, naming and sounding the letters of the alphabet.

L11    Use their phonic knowledge to write simple regular words and make phonetically plausible attempts at more complex words.

L12    Explore and experiment with sounds, words and texts.

L13    Retell narratives in the correct sequence, drawing on language patterns of stories.

L14    Read a range of familiar and common words and simple sentences independently.

L15    Know that print carries meaning and, in English, is read from left to right and top to bottom.

L16    Show an understanding of the elements of stories, such as main character, sequence of events and openings, and how information can be found in non-fiction texts to answer questions about where, who, why and how.

L17    Attempt writing for different purposes, using features of different forms such as lists, stories and instructions.

L18    Write their own names and other things such as labels and captions, and begin to form simple sentences, sometimes using punctuation.

L19    Use a pencil and hold it effectively to form recognisable letters, most of which are correctly formed.

A number of the activities suggested for the theme of 'Shopping' encourage the children to write using their phonic knowledge and to recognise words. They have the opportunity to produce posters, write lists, make price labels and catalogues and fill in cheques. Activities

using fiction, allow the children to enjoy sharing books and to respond in a variety of ways to what they hear, reinforcing and extending their vocabularies. Throughout all the activities the children should be encouraged to interact and to listen.

# Problem Solving, Reasoning and Numeracy (N)

By the end of the EYFS, children should:

N1    Say and use number names in order in familiar contexts.

N2    Count reliably up to ten everyday objects.

N3    Recognise numerals 1 to 9.

N4    Use developing mathematical ideas and methods to solve practical problems.

N5    In practical activities and discussion, begin to use the vocabulary involved in adding and subtracting.

N6    Use language such as 'more' or 'less' to compare two numbers.

N7    Find one more or one less than a number from one to ten.

N8    Begin to relate addition to combining two groups of objects and subtraction to 'taking away'.

N9    Use language such as 'greater', 'smaller', 'heavier' or 'lighter' to compare quantities.

N10    Talk about, recognise and recreate simple patterns.

N11    Use language such as 'circle' or 'bigger' to describe the shape and size of solids and flat shapes.

N12    Use everyday words to describe position.

The theme of 'Shopping' provides a meaningful context for activities that encourage the children to use numbers, to reason and to solve problems. The opportunity to count occurs as children use the 'DIY number rhyme' and role-play buying and selling. Children will explore shapes and size as they compare envelope sizes to 'buy' stamps and sort coins from different countries. Children will recognise numbers when they match shoes to boxes, examine clothes labels for sizes and ages and 'buy' tickets for a holiday.

# Knowledge and Understanding of the World (K)

By the end of the EYFS, children should:

K1    Investigate objects and materials by using all of their senses as appropriate.

K2    Find out about, and identify, some features of living things, objects and events they observe.

K3    Look closely at similarities, differences, patterns and change.

K4    Ask questions about why things happen and how things work.

K5    Build and construct with a wide range of objects, selecting appropriate resources and adapting their work where necessary.

K6    Select the tools and techniques they need to shape, assemble and join materials they are using.

K7    Find out about and identify the uses of everyday technology and use information and communication technology and programmable toys to support their learning.

K8    Find out about past and present events in their own lives, and in those of their families and other people they know.

K9    Observe, find out about and identify features in the place they live and the natural world.

K10    Find out about their environment, and talk about those features they like and dislike.

K11    Begin to know about their own cultures and beliefs and those of other people.

The topic of 'Shopping' offers opportunities for children to make observations, and to compare. As they explore cases and bags for a holiday the children are encouraged to notice details. Activities such as making trolleys and party bags give them the opportunity to select materials and to construct. Through all the activities children should be encouraged to observe, to talk and to give reasons for choices and observations.

# Physical Development (PD)

By the end of the EYFS, children should:

PD1 Move with confidence, imagination and in safety.

PD2 Move with control and coordination.

PD3 Travel around, under, over and through balancing and climbing equipment.

PD4 Show awareness of space, of themselves and of others.

PD5 Recognise the importance of keeping healthy, and those things which contribute to this.

PD6 Recognise the changes that happen to their bodies when they are active.

PD7 Use a range of small and large equipment.

PD8 Handle tools, objects, construction and malleable materials safely and with increasing control.

Activities such as using dough and construction toys will offer experience of PD8. Through pretending to shop and to deliver food children will have the opportunity to move with control and imagination. When playing traditional party games and using a range of small equipment, such as beanbags for hats and hoops as pizzas, the children will be encouraged to develop their co-ordination.

# Creative Development (C)

By the end of the EYFS, children should :

C1 Respond in a variety of ways to what they see, hear, smell, touch and feel.

C2 Express and communicate their ideas, thoughts and feelings by using a widening range of materials, suitable tools, imaginative and role-play, movement, designing and making, and a variety of songs and musical instruments.

C3 Explore colour, texture, shape, form and space in two or three dimensions.

C4 Recognise and explore how sounds can be changed, sing simple songs from memory, recognise repeated sounds and sound patterns and match movements to music.

C5 Use their imagination in art and design, music, dance, imaginative and role-play and stories.

During this topic children will experience working with a variety of materials as they make paper plate hats, models of gardens and collages of T-shirts. They will be able to develop their imaginations and skills of painting, drawing and colouring as they create posters and portraits. Throughout all the activities children should be encouraged to talk about what they see and feel as they communicate their ideas in painting, models, collage work and role-play. When singing songs about clothes and holidays the children will recognise and explore how sounds can be changed.

# Week 1

# Let's go shopping!

## Personal, Social and Emotional Development

- Talk about the different kinds of shop that exist. Encourage the children to explain what they like and dislike about shopping. (PS3, 5)
- Talk about the importance of saying 'please' and 'thank you' when shopping. Enjoy role-play shopping and selling. (PS7, 9)

## Communication, Language and Literacy

- Ask the children to make lists by cutting pictures from catalogues and magazines. Use the lists to play 'I want to buy something that begins/ends with/rhymes with/can be bought from ...' (L2)
- Make cheques for the children to practise writing names and numbers (see activity opposite). (L18)
- Enjoy sharing a book about shopping (see Resources for suggestions). (L3, 4)

## Problem Solving, Reasoning and Numeracy

- Help children to identify the value of coins up to 10 pence and to swap them for 1 pence coins. (N1, 2, 3, 4)
- Explain what PIN numbers are. Write four digits on credit card sized pieces of card. Encourage the children to enjoy typing the digits on large calculators and to read them. (N3)

- Sort objects into shopping bags/baskets by shape, size and colour. Encourage the children to compare the numbers in each set. (N6, 12)

## Knowledge and Understanding of the World

- Make a collection of carrier bags from a variety of shops. Sort them according to their handles, size and strength. Which bags are the most comfortable to carry? Which one would last the longest? Which would be good for carrying tins/books/clothes? (K1, 3)
- Talk about recycling shopping bags and 'bags for life'. Encourage the children to understand why bags should not be wasted. (K4)
- Make shopping trolleys from shoe boxes. Encourage the children to select materials to make wheels that turn. (K5, 6)

## Physical Development

- Use large and small equipment to enjoy playing going shopping. (PD1, 2)
- Use construction toys to make supermarkets. Talk about the types of things that would be sold. Help the children to realise that aisles should be wide for trolleys and wheelchairs to travel and turn, and to give room for items to be displayed. (PD8)

## Creative Development

- Enjoy using the 'Going shopping' song (see activity opposite). (C4, 5)
- Provide large sheets of paper and paint for children to make pictures of shops. (C5)

## Activity: Writing cheques

**Learning opportunity:** Writing names and numbers.

**Early learning goal:** Communication, Language and Literacy. Children should write their own names and other things such as labels and captions...

**Resources:** Catalogues/books with pictures of toys, pencils, real cheque book, role-play cheques.

**Key vocabulary:** Amount, pay, cheque, sign, catalogue, buy, cost.

**Organisation:** Small group.

**What to do:** Show the group the cheque book. Ask whether anyone has seen one before. Talk about cheques and how people used to use them before credit cards were invented. Explain that cheques still can be useful when buying something through the post. Point out the parts that people have to fill in.

Look through the catalogue and together choose something to buy. Demonstrate how to fill in a role-play cheque. Encourage the children to practise writing their names and numbers as they enjoy completing cheques to 'buy' toys from the catalogues or books.

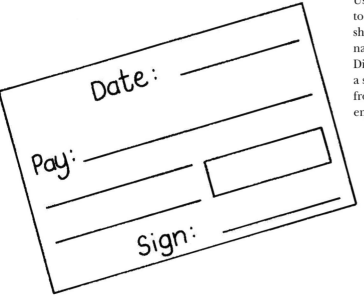

## Activity: The 'Going Shopping Song'

**Learning opportunity:** Singing and adding actions to the words.

**Early learning goal:** Creative Development. Children should ... sing simple songs from memory ... and match movements to music. They should use their imagination in ... music ...

**Resources:** Bag of items that could be bought from a variety of shops, e.g. a toy, trainers, an apple, a book, soap.

**Key vocabulary:** Shopping, buy, names for items bought and shops.

**Organisation:** Whole group.

**What to do:** Sitting on the floor show the children the items in the bag. Ask for ideas of where each item could be bought. Invite a child to select one item. Sing the shopping song to the tune of 'Frère Jacques'. Encourage the children to do actions for each line and provide the name of the shop from which the item was bought. On the final line the child with the item should pass the object to another child. This child then selects the next item to be bought.

Let's go shopping, let's go shopping.
We will buy, we will buy.
Apples from the grocers,
Apples from the grocers,
For *Leanne*, for *Leanne*.

## Display

Use blue wallpaper for sky and grey sugar paper as pavement to make a background for the shop paintings. Cut out the shops and arrange them as a street. Ask children to suggest names for their shops. On a table in front arrange the trolleys. Display pictures of foods with prices from 1 to 20 pence on a small board. Nearby put out role-play cheques, envelopes from junk mail and pencils for the children to continue to enjoy practising writing names and numbers.

# Week 2

# Shopping for food

## Personal, Social and Emotional Development

- As a group, make a list of all the places from which people can buy food. Talk about the kinds of foods that children like to eat. (PS3)
- Remind the children of routines for listening and taking turns. Play 'I went to market and bought …' Encourage the children to take it in turn to add a new food to the list. Use actions as prompts to help children to remember previous foods. (PS8)

## Communication, Language and Literacy

- Use simple recipe books to make lists of ingredients that need to be bought to make buns or biscuits. (L17, 19)
- Read *The Very Hungry Caterpillar* by Eric Carle. Tell the children that they are taking the caterpillar to a café. Make menus of foods that he might like to buy. (L17, 19)

## Problem Solving, Reasoning and Numeracy

- Ask carers to donate fruit for a food stall. Let each child 'spend' up to 10 pence. Encourage children to use positional language as they explain the place of the food they wish to buy (see activity opposite). (N3, 12)
- Use a variety of clean yogurt pots, tubs and food containers in the sand and water trays to role-play food shopping and visiting a café. Encourage the children to buy, to sell, to count and to compare amounts. (N1, 9)

## Knowledge and Understanding of the World

- Investigate foods from around the world. Invite adults from a variety of cultural backgrounds to talk about where they buy the ingredients to make their national dishes (e.g. curry, paella, haggis). (K11)
- Having first checked with carers for details of food allergies, invite children to try a range of unusual fruits from a shopping basket. What do they taste like? Where were the fruits grown? Where can they be bought? (K1, 3)

## Physical Development

- Outside, role-play delivering food. Use hoops as giant pizzas, skittles for milk, balls as fruit and beanbags as bread. (PD1, 7)
- Use malleable materials to make models of foods sold in a supermarket. (PD8)

## Creative Development

- Mix a range of ready-mixed paints with PVA glue. Use thin brushes to paint favourite foods on paper plates. When dry, use some of the plates in a role-play café. (C5)
- Create packets for cereals (see activity opposite). (C3)
- In small groups enjoy arranging clean, empty food packets to make displays for a supermarket or grocery shop. When complete, take digital photos of the displays. (C3)

## Activity: Food for sale

**Learning opportunity:** Recognising numbers and using positional language.

**Early learning goal:** Problem Solving, Reasoning and Numeracy. Children should recognise numerals 1 to 9. They should use everyday words to describe position.

**Resources:** Selection of safe fruits; clean, plastic plates and beakers; price list (e.g. grape 1p, apple 2p); money (50p in 1p coins).

**Key vocabulary:** Names of fruits and numbers; 1 pence coin, cost, how much?

**Organisation:** 2 – 3 children.

**What to do:** Prepare for the activity by checking with carers that the children may eat the fruit. Set out a selection, and cut in pieces, on a plate for each group of children.

Show the children the price list, and depending on the amount of fruit available give each child up to 10 pence. Invite a child to make a choice of a piece of fruit using the price list. Ask how much money will be needed to buy it. Then ask the child to say which piece they would like. Encourage them to use positional language such as 'I would like the piece of apple in the front row. It is next to the grapes.' Once the fruit has been bought and eaten, continue selling and buying until all the pieces have been sold.

# Activity: Making packets for cereals

**Learning opportunity:** Sticking and painting.

**Early learning goal:** Creative Development. Children should explore colour …, texture, shape, form and space in two or three dimensions.

**Resources:** Masking tape, cereal packets, paint and brushes, scissors.

**Key vocabulary:** Names of colours and cereals.

**Organisation:** Small group.

**What to do:** Talk about the foods that people like to buy to eat for breakfast. Look at the empty cereal packets and discuss children's preferences. Explain that sometimes people see new brands in a shop and decide to buy foods because they look exciting/tasty/different.

Demonstrate how to undo a cereal box and remake it inside out using masking tape to secure the edges. Ask the children to paint the boxes as if they were new cereals for children. When dry, ask the children to give their new cereals a name and help them to use ICT to make labels for the packets.

## Display

Cover a display board with green paper for grass. In the middle, put up a paper tablecloth. Arrange some of the paper plates of painted foods on and around the cloth (saving some plates for role-play). Use large boxes, painted or covered with cloth or paper, to display the cereal packets as if in a shop window display.

# Week 3

# Shopping for clothes and shoes

## Personal, Social and Emotional Development

- Enjoy buying and selling clothes in a role-play clothes shop. Encourage the children to use their manners as they buy and sell. (PS7)
- Demonstrate how to fold clothes to put them neatly into carrier bags. Talk about why folding clothes neatly is a useful skill (see activity opposite). (PS9)

## Communication, Language and Literacy

- Make a collection of clothes catalogues. Encourage the children to enjoy filling in simple order forms for a new outfit. (L17, 18, 19)
- Role-play telephone conversations to order clothes for a book character. Encourage the children to look closely at book illustrations to see what the characters would wear and to use descriptive vocabulary as they make their orders. (L1, 2, 7)
- Make catalogues for a particular type of clothing e.g. dresses, trousers, socks. Use pictures from magazines and drawings to illustrate the catalogues. Encourage the children to write labels for the clothes and prices. (L17, 18, 19)

## Problem Solving, Reasoning and Numeracy

- Talk about the ways that feet are measured in shoe shops. Use A4 sized paper with lines to measure feet. Demonstrate how to place the heel on a line and then count how many gaps long the foot is.(N9)

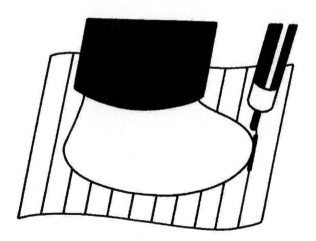

- Talk about the use of labels to help people know which clothes to buy. Sort clothes by age or size, encouraging the children to read the numbers on labels. (N3)
- Make a collection of shoes of varying sizes and labeled boxes or bags. Match the shoes, by size to their corresponding box/bag. (N3)

## Knowledge and Understanding of the World

- Make a collection of clothes hangers from a variety of shops. Help the children to evaluate the use of the hangers. Which ones fit the clothes best? What are they made from? How easy are the skirt/trouser hangers to use? (K1, 3)
- Invite carers to show the children clothes from a range of cultures and styles. Ask them to talk about where and how they bought the clothes. (K11)

## Physical Development

- Talk about big shop sales. Hold dressing up races. Tell the children they are at a sale, the clothes are very cheap and they need to try on and 'buy' the clothes quickly. (PD1, 2)
- Use beanbags as hats. Encourage the children to buy hats and to walk carefully as they wear them home. (PD2, 7)

## Creative Development

- Paint or do collages of new T-shirts for a favourite book character. (C1, 3)
- Make a collection of songs and poems that include clothing (e.g. 'There was an old lady who lived in a shoe (traditional); 'Wayne's got his shoes on the wrong feet' in *Silly Aunt Sally* by Jan Holdstock.) Enjoy reciting/singing them and adding percussion. (C2)
- Make hats out of large paper plates for a hat shop (see activity opposite). (C3)

Planning
for
Learning
through
Shopping

**12** Practical Pre-School

## Activity: Folding clothes

**Learning opportunity:** Appreciating why it is important to take care of clothes.

**Early learning goal:** Personal, Social and Emotional development. Children should understand what is right, what is wrong and why.

**Resources:** A collection of T-shirts, sweatshirts and socks; a creased T-shirt; carrier bags from clothes shops.

**Key vocabulary:** T-shirt, sweatshirt, sock, crease, crumpled, fold, smooth, tidy, care.

**Organisation:** Small group.

**What to do:** Show the group the creased T-shirt. Ask the children why they think it is crumpled. Talk about the need to look after clothes. Demonstrate how to fold a sweatshirt and a T-shirt, and how to roll two socks into a paired bundle. With the children role-play buying and selling clothes. Encourage the children to say 'please' and 'thank you' and to fold clothes carefully before placing them in bags.

## Activity: Hats for special occasions

**Learning opportunity:** Making paper plate hats.

**Early learning goal:** Creative Development. Children should explore colour, texture, shape, form and space in two or three dimensions.

**Resources:** Picture of people wearing hats at a special occasion e.g. wedding, Royal Ascot; felt pens, decorative materials e.g. shiny papers, sequins, flowers, tissue paper, glue, scissors, a paper plate with slits for each child (see diagram) and two ribbons or elastic.

**Key vocabulary:** Hat, decorate, names for colours and materials used.

**Organisation:** Whole group introduction, pairs for the practical activity.

**What to do:** Talk to the children about when hats are worn and the reasons for wearing them. Explain that sometimes they are worn for special occasions such as weddings. Show the children the picture. Ask them to describe the hats. Which hat do the children like best? Why?

Show the children a paper plate and explain that they are each going to make a special hat. Working with pairs of children, help them to colour the plate, to bend upwards the segments and to stick on decoration. The decorative pieces could be flowers/shapes; bits cut from greetings cards/wrapping paper; sequins, scrunched tissue etc. When finished, fix on elastic or ribbons through punched holes.

## Display

Use shoe boxes to set out the hats at varying heights, as if in a hat shop. Put out a range of photos of members of the group and celebrities and invite children to choose hats to buy that would go well with the outfits in the pictures.

Place the T-shirt pictures in large plastic wallets to make a big book. Put the book in the book corner with books containing pictures of the characters for which the shirts were made. Encourage the children to enjoy matching the shirts to their owners.

# Week 4
# Shopping for holidays

### Personal, Social and Emotional Development
- Talk about why some people like to go on holiday. Invite the children to paint pictures of places that they have been to, or would like to visit, for holidays. (PS2, 5)
- Make a collection of pictures of holiday destinations. Help the children to imagine they are buying a holiday. Ask them to select a picture and to explain why they would like to visit that place. (PS4)

### Communication, Language and Literacy
- Make holiday brochures. (L11, 17, 18, 19)
- Write lists of things that would need to be bought for a holiday to a particular place (e.g. sunscreen for a visit to a hot country or to go skiing; comfy shoes/ boots for a walking holiday). (L11, 17, 18, 19)
- Make sun safety posters for the role-play travel agents (see creative development). (L11, 17, 18, 19)

### Problem Solving, Reasoning and Numeracy
- Use a collection of foreign coins for sorting, counting and size activities. (N1, 2, 6)
- Make train and plane tickets from scraps of cards.

Write a number from 1 to 10 on each ticket and the name of the destination. Encourage the children to enjoy buying and selling the tickets using 1, 2, 5 and 10 pence coins. Where appropriate, show the children how to work out the change. (N1, 2, 8)

### Knowledge and Understanding of the World
- Invite a carer to talk to the group about their preparations to visit another country. Encourage the children to ask questions about how tickets for travel are bought. (K4)
- Make a collection of cases and bags that people might buy to take on holiday. Examine their special features. Use a box to size them as suitable/ unsuitable for hand luggage on a plane (see activity opposite). (K1, 3)

### Physical Development
- Label five seaside buckets with prices from one to five pence. Encourage children to 'buy' a bucket by aiming beanbags or small balls into them. Who spends the most money? (PD7)

- Tell a story about shopping to go on a skiing holiday for children to role-play. If large equipment is available enjoy walking over and under bridges, climbing ladders to find equipment and balancing as the children pretend to try on skis and snow-boots. (PD1, 2, 3)

## Creative Development

- Set up the role-play area as a travel agents. Encourage the children to be both tourists and travel agents as they plan and buy holidays for both the winter and summer seasons. (C5)
- Make suitcases from pieces of A4 card folded in half. Inside draw and colour things, or cut items from catalogues, that would need to be bought for the holiday. (C5)

## Activity: Sun safety protection posters

**Learning opportunity:** Writing for a purpose (sun safety).

**Early learning goal:** Communication, Language and Literacy. Children should use their phonic knowledge to write simple regular words and make phonetically plausible attempts at more complex words. They should attempt writing for different purposes, using features of different forms such as lists, stories and instructions. They should write their own names and other things such as labels and captions ... They should use a pencil and hold it effectively to form recognisable letters, most of which are correctly formed.

**Resources:** A3 pieces of paper, crayons, felt pens, pencils, sunscreen, sunglasses, T-shirt with sleeves, bottle of water.

**Key vocabulary:** Sunglasses, sunscreen, protection, sun, safe.

**Organisation:** Whole group.

**What to do:** Talk to the children about the need to take special precautions when going out in the sun. Ask for suggestions of things to do. These might include staying in the shade between 11:00am and 3:00pm; wearing a sunhat, T-shirt with sleeves and sunglasses; and using sunscreen.

Tell the children that sun safety posters are needed for the role-play travel agents. Give each child a piece of paper and ask them to make posters that show people what to do when it is sunny. Show them items such as a sunhat, sunglasses and a bottle of sunscreen to encourage them to draw and colour recognizable pictures. Explain that posters should be simple, not too cluttered, and eye catching.

## Activity: Buying bags

**Learning opportunity:** Observing luggage to find similarities and differences and measuring.

**Early learning goal:** Knowledge and Understanding of the World. Children should investigate objects and materials by using all of their senses as appropriate. They should look closely at similarities, differences ...

**Resources:** Collection of suitcases, rucksacks and bags; box of a similar size to hand luggage on a plane.

**Key vocabulary:** Luggage, suitcase, rucksack, bag, measure, size, names for the materials from which the luggage is made.

**Organisation:** Whole group.

**What to do:** Talk about luggage that people take on holiday. Explain that depending on where you go, what you do and how you travel different bags/cases will be needed. Sometimes people buy luggage because they need lots of space or a small bag to be hand luggage on a plane.

Examine the cases and bags. Encourage the children to feel the materials, the weight of each piece of luggage and how easy it is to carry/wheel. Talk about the kinds of places where each one might be taken. Invite ideas for a place to go on holiday and a way to travel. Ask the children to select the most suitable luggage for that holiday. Finish by letting the children imagine they need to buy a bag for hand luggage on a plane. Encourage them to place each bag in a hand luggage sized box in order to find ones that are suitable.

## Display

Hang up suns cut from shiny or orange card interspersed with strips of orange and yellow crepe paper. Nearby display the sun protection posters. On a table place a box containing an empty plastic bottle of sunscreen, plastic sunglasses, a water bottle and a sunhat.

# Week 5
# Shopping for birthdays

## Personal, Social and Emotional Development
● Talk about ways to celebrate birthdays. (PS5)
● In pairs role-play shopping for a doll's or a soft toy's birthday. Provide paper, old greetings cards, small gifts, toy foods etc. for the children to select props for their playing. (PS12)

## Communication, Language and Literacy
● Talk about the kinds of shops that are useful for birthday celebrations. Where could ingredients for a cake, or a birthday cake be bought? Which shops are good for buying presents and cards? (L2)
● In groups make up stories about shopping for a birthday celebration. (L6)
● Involve the children in finding books that mention birthdays for a birthday book box. Talk about the kinds of things that would need to be bought for any birthday celebrations mentioned in the books. (L4)

## Problem Solving, Reasoning and Numeracy
● Decorate birthday biscuits with ingredients 'bought' for up to 10 pence (see activity opposite). (N3, 5)
● Set out a role-play area as a card shop. Provide used birthday cards for the children to buy and sell. Encourage the children to choose cards for specific people or toys. (N4)

Happy Birthday to you . . . .

- Use a post office size chart to sort birthday cards into 'letter', 'large letter' and 'packet' sizes. Encourage the children to use size vocabulary and to 'buy' the correct stamps. (N11)

## Knowledge and Understanding of the World
- Make and decorate birthday buns. (K1)
- Make party bags (see activity opposite). (K1, 6)

## Physical Development
- Enjoy playing traditional party games. (PD2)
- Talk about entertainments that are sometimes hired for birthday parties such as clowns and bouncy castles. Enjoy role playing being a clown juggling or bouncing on a mat. (PD1)

## Creative Development
- Show the children pictures of party outfits. Discuss which they would buy for a fancy dress party if they had money. Encourage the children to paint portraits of themselves wearing new party clothes. (C5)
- Sing 'Happy birthday to you' to include something bought (e.g. Happy birthday *Connie*, Happy birthday *Connie*. We've bought you a *doll's pram*, Happy birthday *Connie*.) Choose children to suggest a present and a named child to mime receiving the gift. (C4)

# Activity: Decorating party biscuits

**Learning opportunity:** Working out costs and recognising numbers.

**Early learning goal:** Problem Solving, Reasoning and Numeracy. Children should recognise numerals 1 to 9. They should, in practical activities and discussion, begin to use the vocabulary involved in adding and subtracting.

**Resources:** Plain biscuits, tube icing, small sweets, sprinkles, table covers, aprons, paper plates, cards with prices from 1 to 4 pence.

**Key vocabulary:** Numerals 1 to 9, names for biscuit decorations.

**Organisation:** Pairs of children.

**What to do:** Prepare for the activity by checking with carers that their children may handle/eat the foods to be used. Ensure that safe, hygienic procedures are followed for the biscuit decorating. Set out the materials to be used with prices of 1 – 3 pence. Price the tube icing at 4 pence.

Explain to the children that they have 10 pence to spend on icing for a party biscuit. Show the children the

available decoration. Demonstrate how to squeeze the icing from the end of the tube and how it can be used to stick on sweets/sprinkles. Invite the children, in turn, to spend up to 10 pence on ingredients. Leave the biscuits to set on named paper plates.

# Activity: Making party bags

**Learning opportunity:** Investigating materials and making bags.

**Early learning goal:** Knowledge and Understanding of the World. Children should investigate objects and materials by using all of their senses as appropriate. They should select the tools and techniques they need to … join materials they are using.

**Resources:** Examples of bought party bags, A4 and A3 paper, pens, crayons, decorative materials/stickers, stapler, glue, tape, scissors.

**Key vocabulary:** Party bag, names for materials and tools.

**Organisation:** Whole group introduction, small group practical activity.

**What to do:** Show the children the bought party bags. Ask if anyone has ever received one. Encourage the children to look closely at the way the bags have been made, their size and strength. Which bag do the children like best? Why? Where can party bags be bought? Could bags be made instead?

Invite small groups to select materials and tools to make a party bag. When complete, encourage the children to compare the way the bags have been made and decorated. Place the finished bags in the role-play card shop.

# Display
Cover a board with black paper. Put up a safe mirror at child height, and arrange the portraits around it. In a nearby box place a selection of dressing up clothes for the children to 'buy' to dress like one of the portraits.

# Week 6

# At the DIY store

## Personal, Social and Emotional Development

- Tell the children that DIY means 'do it yourself'. Explain what a DIY store is and encourage the children to talk of visits to DIY stores and things they have seen their carers do for themselves at home. (PS1, 3)
- Look in picture books for illustrations showing insides of homes. Invite suggestions of DIY jobs that might improve the rooms/homes such as redecorating or adding a sink. (PS5)

## Communication, Language and Literacy

- Play Kim's game with a variety of safe objects that could be bought at a DIY store. (i.e. Place objects on a tray, let children look at them for a minute, cover the tray and then see how many objects can be remembered.) (L2)
- Give each child a box like a shoebox to make into a bedroom. Help the children to write lists of the materials they will need to transform the boxes (see Knowledge and Understanding of the World). (L11)
- Make posters for the table top sale (see page 20). (L11)

## Problem Solving, Reasoning and Numeracy

- Talk about buying flat pack furniture and the importance of checking the number of pieces before starting to build. Provide small quantities of a construction toy. Encourage the children to sort similar pieces into groups and to count their numbers. (N2)
- Enjoy using the tower building rhyme (see activity opposite). (N1, 2, 8)

## Knowledge and Understanding of the World

- Provide a variety of shapes cut from cereal packets for the children to cover with wallpaper or wrapping paper and practise the skills of cutting and gluing. (K6)
- Provide wallpaper scraps, fabric scraps, small boxes etc. for children to do DIY and turn shoe boxes into bedrooms. (K5, 6)

## Physical Development

- Talk about the kinds of games people can buy to play outside. Provide cereal packets, plastic pots, tubes and balls for the children to make their own aiming and target throwing games. Once made encourage the children to enjoy playing the games (see activity opposite). (PD7)
- Use large apparatus to enjoy role-play buying paint and wallpaper and then doing the painting and decorating. (PD3)

## Creative Development

- Talk about the kinds of things that can be bought from garden centres. In shallow, plastic dishes make model gardens. Use milk carton lids as fishponds, lolly sticks for fences, shells/pebbles for rockeries, twigs as trees etc. (C3, 5)
- Look at a range of sizes of paint brushes. Discuss which ones would be bought for painting walls. Which ones would be best for window frames? Enjoy using large brushes to paint with water on the playground. (C3)

## Activity: DIY number rhyme

**Learning opportunity:** Counting and adding.

**Early learning goal:** Problem Solving, Reasoning and Numeracy. Children should: say and use number names in order in familiar contexts; count reliably up to ten everyday objects; begin to relate addition to combining two groups of objects ...

**Resources:** Twenty toy building blocks.

**Key vocabulary:** Numbers to ten/twenty; DIY, tower, high, block, tall.

**Organisation:** Small group.

**What to do:** Talk about DIY and the kinds of things that some people build. Explain that you want to build a tower six blocks high. Together build the tower. Stand back and look carefully at the tower. Then say that you think it could be higher. Place two more blocks on and ask the children to say how tall the tower is now. Recite the rhyme encouraging the children to do actions for building and measuring the tower, and to hold up fingers to show the numbers.

Let's do DIY
Build a tower (*insert number*) blocks high;
Count them starting from the floor
Oh no it needs (*insert number*) blocks more.
How tall will it be?
This tower I have built for me.

Repeat the rhyme with different numbers. Encourage the children to work out how many bricks high the tower is once others are added on.

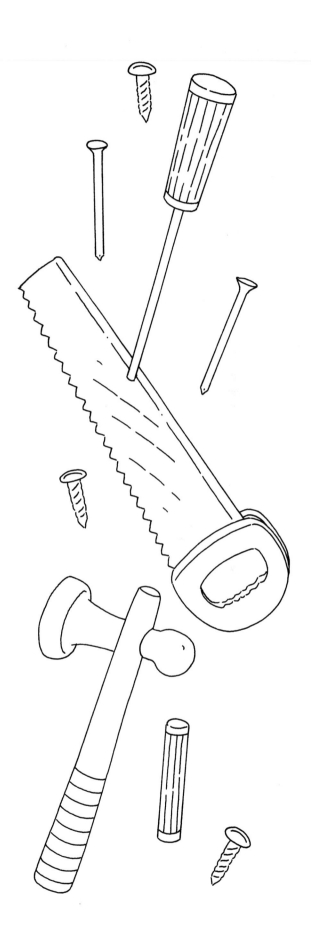

## Activity: DIY games

**Learning opportunity:** Inventing games and using small equipment.

**Early learning goal:** Physical Development. Children should use a range of small equipment …

**Resources:** Beanbags, balls, small bats, hoops, boxes, cardboard tubes, hoopla game.

**Key vocabulary:** Names for the games and resources used.

**Organisation:** Whole group.

**What to do:** Talk to the children about games they like to play outside. Tell them you have just bought a game to play outside and show the children the hoopla set. Demonstrate how to play it. Explain that it costs money to buy the hoopla set but games can also be made. Invite pairs of children to select resources to invent their own games.

## Display

Put out the shoe box rooms and gardens with name labels made by the children. Write out the DIY Number Rhyme and place it on a table with a box of toy bricks and a large die. Encourage children to use the die to select a number for the height of the tower to build and to enjoy using the rhyme independently.

# Bringing It All Together - Table Top Sale

A table top sale is an excellent way to raise funds, for the group or a charity, at the same time as helping children and their carers to 'de-clutter' and make money for themselves. It also gives the children the chance to experience one more aspect of shopping. Encourage carers to include their children in sorting things to sell and in writing price tags for the items.

The sale involves carers renting a table for a given amount. They can then set up and run a stall, with their children, of unwanted possessions. Any money raised by the carers is theirs. Thus the group will gain the table rent plus money raised through selling refreshments and running their own stall. Carers are responsible for their own areas including setting out and clearing away. They also need to remember to bring a container for money and to be able to give change for purchases.

## Preparation

Publish the date for the forthcoming table top sale well in advance of the shopping topic. In week 1 of the topic, send a letter home outlining how the sale will be organised with a reply slip for carers to book a table and to send in their non-returnable rent. Make a plan to show the space to be used and tables. As people book a table, write their name on the plan. Some families may wish to share a table.

Involve the children in decorating name signs for their carers' tables and in making posters about the sale. On the day before the sale help the children to decorate plain biscuits for a refreshment stall and reminder notes to take home about the next day's sale.

## The Table Top Sale

Hold the sale on a Saturday to maximize the number of people who can attend. Ensure the tables are sufficiently spaced out for people to buy without pushing and that the names of the stall holders are clearly displayed. For safety, keep the refreshments away from the table top sale area and provide chairs for the weary shoppers!

Table top sales are great fun. They require minimal organisation but can bring much enjoyment to children and their families as the Shopping topic is given a real purpose.

# Resources

## Resources to collect
- Plastic carriers (NB check that they have safety air holes)
- Resources for a role-play food shop, café, travel agents and clothes shop e.g. telephone, cash register, clothes, shoe boxes, travel brochures, catalogues, money
- Long cardboard tubes
- Junk mail envelopes
- Cress seeds
- Beanbags
- Suitcases, rucksacks and hold-alls
- Coins from a range of countries

## Everyday resources:
- Boxes e.g. cereal packets, shoe boxes, a large box of plane hand-luggage size
- Variety of papers and cards e.g. sugar, tissue, silver and shiny papers, wallpaper, corrugated card etc.
- Paint, different sized paint brushes and a variety of paint mixing containers
- Pencils, crayons, pastels, felt pens etc.
- Glue and scissors
- Decorative and finishing materials such as sequins, foils, glitter, tinsel, shiny wool and threads, beads, pieces of textiles, parcel ribbon
- Materials to make wheels and axles e.g. cotton reels, card wheels, dowel, wooden clothes pegs etc.
- Table covers
- Malleable materials such as play-dough
- Playground chalk
- Masking tape

All of the following books were available from leading booksellers at the time of writing. When planning for the topic, however, look through the books already within your setting. It is likely that you will find good alternatives to the suggested books.

## Books for children
- Janet and Allan Ahlberg *The Baby's Catalogue* (Puffin)
- Eileen Browne *Handa's Surprise* (Walker Books)
- John Burningham *The Shopping Basket* (Red Fox)
- Eric Carle *The Very Hungry Caterpillar* (Picture Puffins)
- Julia Donaldson *The Smartest Giant in Town* (Macmillan)
- Sally Gardner *Fairy Shopping* (Dolphin Paperbacks)
- Jane Hissey *The Old Bear* series (Red Fox)
- Shirley Hughes *Alfie and the Birthday Surprise* (Red Fox)
- Jane Kemp and Clare Walters *My First Toy Catalogue* (Oxford University Press)
- Mandy Stanley *Lettice The Birthday Party* (HarperCollins Children's Books)

## Resources for planning
- Department for Education and Skills (2007) *The Early Years Foundation Stage Setting the Standards for Learning, Development and Care for children from birth to five.* Department for Education and Skills, London
- For additional ideas linking with the 'Shopping' theme see the following titles within the *Planning for Learning Series* (Step Forward Publishing):
- *Clothes*
- *Toys*
- *What are things made from?* (Bringing it all together – The jumble sale)

# Collecting Evidence of Children's Learning

**Monitoring children's development is an important task. Keeping a record of children's achievements, interests and learning styles will help you to see progress and will draw attention to those who are having difficulties for some reason. If a child needs additional professional help, such as speech therapy, your records will provide valuable evidence.**

Records should cover all the areas of learning and be the result of collaboration between group leaders, parents and carers. Parents should be made aware of your record keeping policies when their child joins your group. Show them the type of records you are keeping and make sure they understand that they have an opportunity to contribute. As a general rule, your records should form an open document. Any parent should have access to records relating to his or her child. Take regular opportunities to talk to parents about children's progress. If you have formal discussions regarding children about whom you have particular concerns, a dated record of the main points should be kept.

## Keeping it manageable

Records should be helpful in informing group leaders, adult helpers and parents and always be for the benefit of the child. The golden rule is to keep them simple, manageable and useful.

Observations will basically fall into three categories:

## Spontaneous records:

Sometimes you will want to make a note of observations as they happen e.g. a child is heard counting cars accurately during a play activity, or is seen to play collaboratively for the first time.

## Planned observations:

Sometimes you will plan to make observations of children's developing skills in their everyday activities. Using the learning opportunity identified for an activity will help you to make appropriate judgments about children's capabilities and to record them systematically.

To collect information:
- talk to children about their activities and listen to their responses;
- listen to children talking to each other;
- observe children's work such as early writing, drawings, paintings and 3D models. (Keeping photocopies or photographs can be useful.)

Sometimes you may wish to set up 'one-off' activities for the purposes of monitoring development. Some groups at the beginning of each term, for example, ask children to write their name and to make a drawing of themselves to record their progressing skills in both co-ordination and observation. Do not attempt to make records following every activity!

## Reflective observations:

It is useful to spend regular time reflecting on the children's progress. Aim to make some comments about each child each week.

## Informing your planning

Collecting evidence about children's progress is time consuming and it is important that it is useful. When you are planning, use the information you have collected to help you to decide what learning opportunities you need to provide next for children. For example, a child who has poor pencil or brush control will benefit from more play with dough or construction toys to build the strength of hand muscles.

## Example of recording chart

| Name: Edmund Sparks | | D.O.B. 1.2.04 | | | Date of entry: 13.9.07 | |
|---|---|---|---|---|---|---|
| **Term** | **Personal, Social and Emotional Development** | **Communication, Language and Literacy** | **Problem solving, Reasoning and Numeracy** | **Knowledge and Understanding of the World** | **Physical Development** | **Creative Development** |
| **ONE** | Happy to say good-bye to mother. Enjoys both independent and collaborative play. 20.9.07 LBS | Enjoying listening to and retelling stories – excellent memory for details and phrases. Can write first name and simple CVC words. Good pencil grip. 2.10.07 CCM | Is able to say and recognise numbers to ten and to count accurately five objects. Enjoyed counting blocks in the DIY Rhyme. 25.9.07 EHL | Very eager to ask questions always wants to know 'Why?' Keen to learn about clothes from different cultures. 16.10.07 LSS | Very flexible. Can balance on one leg. Loved miming decorating. Good at aiming. Does not like the feel of play-dough. 9.10.07 SJS | Enjoys painting and particularly when mixing own colours. Portrait showed attention to detail. Not keen to get hands messy. 22.10.07 REL |
| **TWO** | | | | | | |
| **THREE** | | | | | | |

Planning for Learning through Shopping

22    Practical Pre-School

# Skills overview of six-week plan

| Week | Topic Focus | Personal, Social and Emotional Development | Communication, Language and Literacy | Problem Solving, Reasoning and Numeracy | Knowledge and Understanding of the World | Physical Development | Creative Development |
|---|---|---|---|---|---|---|---|
| 1 | Let's go shopping | Speaking; Initiating ideas; Showing interest; Understanding what is right and wrong and why; Collaborating | Listening; Writing | Counting; Sorting; Comparing; Recognising numbers | Making observations; Investigating; Talking; Selecting tools and techniques; Constructing | Using large and small equipment; Using construction materials | Singing; Painting |
| 2 | Shopping for food | Maintaining attention; Collaborating | Responding to stories; Writing | Counting; Comparing; Recognising numbers; Using positional language | Comparing; Describing; Investigating; Knowledge of cultures | Moving with imagination and in safety; Using small equipment; Using malleable materials | Painting; Role-play; Making a display |
| 3 | Shopping for clothes and shoes | Understanding what is right and wrong and why; Forming good relationships | Exploring sounds; Role-play; Writing | Sorting; Counting; Recognising numbers; Comparing sizes | Comparing; Investigating; Asking questions; Knowledge of cultures | Moving with control, co-ordination, imagination and in safety; Using small equipment | Painting; Collage; Sticking; Singing |
| 4 | Shopping for holidays | Developing confidence; Showing feelings and sensitivity to needs | Using phonic knowledge to write words | Counting; Recognising numbers; Comparing | Observing; Comparing; Asking questions | Moving with imagination, control, co-ordination and in safety; Throwing and aiming | Role-play; Cutting and sticking |
| 5 | Shopping for birthdays | Showing awareness of needs; Selecting resources independently | Responding to a story; Writing; Speaking | Counting; Recognising numbers; Sorting by size; Solving problems | Investigating; Selecting tools and techniques | Moving with confidence, imagination, control, co-ordination and in safety | Singing; Painting |
| 6 | At the DIY store | Being interested and motivated; Maintaining attention; Forming good relationships | Speaking; Listening; Using phonic knowledge to write words | Counting; Beginning to add and subtract | Selecting tools and techniques; Constructing | Using large equipment; Throwing and aiming | Painting; Making models |

# Home links

The theme of shopping lends itself to useful links with children's homes and families. Through working together children and adults gain respect for each other and build comfortable and confident relationships.

## Establishing Partnerships
- Keep parents informed about the topic of 'Shopping' and the themes for each week. By understanding the work of the group, parents will enjoy the involvement of contributing ideas, time and resources.
- Photocopy the parent's page for each child to take home. Also send home a note to invite parents to participate in the table top sale and to book a table.
- Invite friends, child minders and families to share in the table top sale.

## Visiting Enthusiasts
- Invite adults from a range of cultures to talk to the group about shopping for foods and clothes.
- Invite a local shopkeeper to explain how he/she organises his/her shop.

## Resource Requests
- Catalogues, shoe boxes, cardboard tubes, cereal packets, greetings cards, colour supplement magazines, wallpaper and wrapping paper are invaluable for creative activities.
- Ask parents to donate:
  clothes hangers and carriers from a variety of shops;
  items for role play areas such as toy foods, dressing up clothes;
  unwanted shoes with their sizes labelled clearly.

## The Table Top Sale
- The table top sale depends on the involvement of parents running stalls and providing items to sell. In addition to requesting their time, ask parents for small, child-friendly items that they would be willing to give to a group stall. On the day, ask for donations of refreshments.